REMARKABLE BUSINESS
VOLUME 2

I love you Dad!

James

REMARKABLE BUSINESS
VOLUME 2

SPOTLIGHTS ON TOP PROFESSIONALS AND BUSINESS OWNERS

LEADING PROFESSIONALS AND BUSINESS OWNERS

FEATURING:

Devon Vince & Nicole Ryan
Julie Lineberger
Mechelle Tucker
Karen Yee
George Dandridge Jr.
Cam Callender
Diane Strand
Kelly Scott
Jenny Ambrose
Showleh Tolbert

Copyright © 2021 Remarkable Press™

All rights reserved. No part of this publication may be reproduced, distributed, or transmitted in any form or by any means, including photocopying, recording, or other electronic or mechanical methods, without the prior written, dated, and signed permission of the authors and publisher, except as provided by the United States of America copyright law.

The information presented in this book represents the views of the author as of the date of publication. The author reserves the right to alter and update their opinions based on new conditions. This book is for informational purposes only.

The author and the publisher do not accept any responsibilities for any liabilities resulting from the use of this information. While every attempt has been made to verify the information provided here, the author and the publisher cannot assume any responsibility for errors, inaccuracies, or omissions. Any similarities with people or facts are unintentional.

Remarkable Business Volume 2/ Mark Imperial —1st ed.
Managing Editor/ Shannon Buritz

ISBN: 978-1-954757-03-5

Remarkable Press™

Royalties from the retail sales of **"REAL ESTATE INSIGHTS: CONVERSATIONS WITH AMERICA'S LEADING REAL ESTATE PROFESSIONALS"** are donated to the Global Autism Project:

AUTISM KNOWS NO BORDERS; FORTUNATELY NEITHER DO WE.®

The Global Autism Project 501(C)3 is a nonprofit organization that provides training to local individuals in evidence-based practice for individuals with autism.

The Global Autism Project believes that every child has the ability to learn, and their potential should not be limited by geographical bounds.

The Global Autism Project seeks to eliminate the disparity in service provision seen around the world by providing high-quality training to individuals providing services in their local community. This training is made sustainable through regular training trips and contiguous remote training.

You can learn more about the Global Autism Project and make direct donations by visiting **GlobalAutismProject.org.**

CONTENTS

A Note to the Reader ix

Introduction.. xi

Devon Vince and Nicole Ryan.. 1

Julie Lineberger 15

Mechelle Tucker 29

Karen Yee 41

George Dandridge Jr. 51

Cam Callender 65

Diane Strand 75

Kelly Scott 89

Jenny Ambrose 105

Showleh Tolbert 119

About the Publisher.. 131

A NOTE TO THE READER

Thank you for buying your copy of "REMARKABLE BUSINESS VOLUME 2: Spotlights on Top Professionals and Business Owners." This book was originally created as a series of live interviews; that's why it reads like a series of conversations, rather than a traditional book that talks at you.

I wanted you to feel as though the participants and I are talking with you, much like a close friend or relative, and felt that creating the material this way would make it easier for you to grasp the topics and put them to use quickly, rather than wading through hundreds of pages.

So relax, grab a pen and paper, take notes, and get ready to learn some fascinating Remarkable Business strategies.

Warmest regards,

Mark Imperial
Publisher, Author, and Radio Personality

INTRODUCTION

"REMARKABLE BUSINESS VOLUME 2: Spotlights on Top Professionals and Business Owners" is a collaborative book series featuring leading professionals from across the country.

Remarkable Press™ would like to extend a heartfelt thank you to all participants who took the time to submit their chapter and offer their support in becoming ambassadors for this project.

100% of the royalties from this book's retail sales will be donated to the Global Autism Project. Should you want to make a direct donation, visit their website at GlobalAutismProject.org

DEVON VINCE AND NICOLE RYAN

DEVON VINCE AND NICOLE RYAN

CONVERSATION WITH DEVON VINCE AND NICOLE RYAN

> Devon, you are the Owner and Head Grower at Hemp Quest Farms. Nicole, you are the Creative Director and Cannabis Nurse Consultant. Tell us about Hemp Quest Farms and the people you help.

Devon Vince: We are a genuine farm-to-table hemp company. We started in 2018 by growing clones for other farms, primarily indoors. I was also doing consulting work for many other farms in the area. After noticing a lack of high-quality CBD full-spectrum products in our area, we took Hemp Quest in a different direction and closed the indoor grow. We partnered with Patterson Farm, located here locally in Mount Ulla, North Carolina. They are an incredible family-owned farm that has served our community for over 100 years. We work exclusively with them. I work with their fourth-generation grandson, Taylor, and we take care of the hemp at their facilities. We have about 12 greenhouses that we can expand into. We are not using all 12 at this time, but we are growing from year to year as things move in our area.

> **Who were you serving back in 2018, and how has your business changed with the expanding legalization of marijuana?**

Devon Vince: In 2018, we were getting all of our infrastructures in place. As soon as 2019 hit, we started growing indoors, and we were able to sell plants directly to farms that were just getting into the marketplace. So the first year, we primarily were in the fields growing for extracts so that people could make CBD oils. Many companies were making their own brands at that time. At the end of 2019, we started to see a lack of transparency. Companies were not showing where the products were coming from. They were not testing everything. So that is when we decided to join Patterson Farms and work with them exclusively to make sure that we controlled everything and produced high-quality products that were safe for everyone to use.

> **What are the challenges people face in trying to find the best sources?**

Devon Vince: In the beginning, all of these stores were popping up. They were buying oils from "who knows where," and there weren't a lot of test results that you could see. As we started growing, we realized the best opportunity was to use our local testing facilities to test every product before it goes to market. We are proud to show that. If you are trying CBD and are not using Hemp Quest Farms, know that there are many good companies out there. Unfortunately, many do not have testing to prove their product is what it says on the bottle. They also don't reveal any pesticides, heavy metals, or molds within the product. If you decide to go with a company other than Hemp Quest Farms, we advise you to ask for information like that. If they are open and transparent, they should be happy to show you the test results.

> **Nicole, as Creative Director and Cannabis Nurse Consultant, tell us about your role at Hemp Quest Farms.**

Nicole Ryan: I'm a jack of all trades. Whatever Devon needs me to do, I make it happen for the company. Most of my role consists of collecting evidence-based practice from my fellow healthcare professionals to ensure the products are safe and effective. The jury is still out on many of the components of cannabis because of the current Schedule 1 status that has been on it for so long. With restrictions slowly being lifted, we are getting more evidence as to what this plant can do. The information is just flooding in. I collaborate with other professionals who have been in the industry for a long time to create educational materials for our clients and guide them on a journey to achieve wellness through the cannabis plant.

> **What are some of the applications and benefits of cannabis?**

Nicole Ryan: Cannabis has been part of our culture for thousands and thousands of years. We almost can't talk about cannabis benefits without first discussing the Endocannabinoid System. The Endocannabinoid System, or ECS, was discovered by Dr. Raphael Mechoulam in the 1960s. This system is essential because it acts as the umbrella to all body systems. The ECS is super complex and has an extensive receptor system that is responsible for maintaining homeostasis within our bodies. Endocannabinoids are produced within our body and attach to these receptors, essentially a neurotransmitter. Cannabinoids, components found in cannabis, act similarly to these neurotransmitters that our own body creates and enhances the body's ability to heal itself on a chemical level. It is not just covering up a symptom of an illness but instead healing from deep within. Evidence shows that anxiety, insomnia, and pain can be relieved with full-spectrum cannabinoid-rich products.

What are some of the different forms?

Devon Vince: There are many different delivery methods for cannabis. Some people like to smoke cannabis or hemp. You can smoke a full spectrum flower with all of the components in it, especially if you get something from our farm that hasn't gone through a lot of hands. However, we feel the most effective for long-term use is to use a sublingual tincture. This works very well within the body. People can also add topicals such as creams, salves, or balms to their routine. For example, if someone has arthritis, they may take the oil one or two times per day and then add a topical if they have a flare-up. We're not a big proponent of vaping, but some people choose to go that route so they can use it on lunch breaks at work or in similar situations where they want to be discreet. You can also find edibles, capsules, patches, and gels.

> **What are some of the biggest myths and misconceptions that exist about cannabis?**

Nicole Ryan: A big misconception is that cannabis is addictive. There is still a lot of debate on this topic. Let's face it; there is potential to abuse ANY medication or substance. But with cannabis use, the risk for addiction is low, it is very safe, and you cannot overdose on it. Another misconception is that all medicinal cannabis products get you high. Hemp Quest products are all full-spectrum, cannabinoid-rich, and contain 0.3% THC, which is the amount of THC legally allowed in North Carolina. There is no "high" feeling, but you may feel more relaxed. Many people don't like the feeling of being "high" or "elevated," and we respect that. I believe small doses of THC can be very therapeutic. We always tell our clients to go "slow and low" with any type of cannabis product so they can learn how it interacts with their body. Everyone is different. One person might take a CBD or full-spectrum hemp oil and get results in one week, while another may take one or two months to see results. Finding the right product and achieving the desired result may take some time. As a nurse, I rely on the nursing process to guide me while providing patient-centered care. My clients will keep a journal to track their use and how they feel before and after to pinpoint what regimen is working for them. Some people choose to use cannabis products like a supplement since it can be very beneficial in maintaining optimal health.

Even if you don't have conditions like insomnia or anxiety, it can contribute to overall well-being.

> **What inspired you to start Hemp Quest Farms?**

Devon Vince: Cannabis has been in my life for many years, and it has helped me in a lot of ways. I jumped at the opportunity to be able to grow this incredible plant in North Carolina. It has been exciting to get involved with like-minded individuals and make quality products for people. There are just so many misconceptions, and people can be apprehensive about trying cannabis because of the lack of information out there. Education is key here. It's very nice to be able to help our local community. People can call us with questions, and we have multiple avenues of reaching out to the community and providing education.

Nicole Ryan: Like Devon said, cannabis has helped him throughout his life. It is gratifying to hear clients say, "Hey, I can't believe this little oil got me to sleep at night. I had the best day today. I wasn't stressed out at work. I was more interactive with my family." One client, in particular, is the driving force behind my passion. She is a young girl with a very rare, fatal genetic disorder called Sanfilippo Syndrome. It is neurodegenerative, and one day she will lose all speech and mobility. There is no cure or treatment. Her mother was searching for a non-conventional way to help her. She started purchasing our oil after doing some research. I couldn't wait to see how the oil would help her. After hearing and reading about how cannabis has helped with other neurodegenerative conditions, I was hoping for at least some relief for this child. Recently I spoke with her mom and asked how her treatment was going, and she said, "For months, we stopped getting smiles and giggles. Hemp Quest CBD has helped bring them back. We are so grateful to you for giving our daughter back her sparkle." That right there means everything to me. It gives you the big picture of what cannabinoid therapeutics can do for people. If you are interested in supporting the fight to cure Sanfilippo Syndrome, check out Aislinnswish.org.

> **How do people find you and connect with you?**

Devon Vince: The pandemic has caused people to reach out to us directly, rather than going into the retail locations that carry our products. This was great for us because we were able to educate people one-on-one and guide them to the best products for them. You can email us directly at Hempquestfarms.com, and from there, we can set up an appointment for a consultation to speak with Nicole or me. If you're in North Carolina, you can find us set up at Patterson Farm on the weekends from mid-April through early June and at The Mint Hill Historical Society's Farmers Market June through September. You can also find us on YouTube, Facebook, and Instagram.

DEVON VINCE

Owner and Head Grower at Hemp Quest Farms

Devon Vince has been a cannabis enthusiast and advocate for over two decades. He founded his company, Hemp Quest Farms, in 2018 and has solidified his space in the cannabis industry. Devon has traveled extensively throughout North Carolina, Oregon, and Colorado to work with growers, seed producers, and equipment manufacturers in order to learn the best practices and procedures for growing cannabis. He believes with knowledge, hard work, and perseverance, we can change the cannabis industry for the better and solidify North Carolina as a premier state for high-quality medicinal hemp, top-shelf cannabinoid-rich products, and well-educated retailers. Devon's goal is to provide his clients safe, affordable, high-quality products that they can rely on for consistency.

Devon resides in Harrisburg, NC, with his son, Mateo, his longtime girlfriend, and their dog, Mary. He enjoys traveling, riding his motorcycle, working in the garden, cooking meals for family and friends, and watching spectacular fireworks displays.

WEBSITE:
https://hempquestfarms.com

EMAIL:
devon@hempquestfarms.com

FACEBOOK:
Hemp Quest Farms

INSTAGRAM:
@HempQuestFarms

NICOLE RYAN

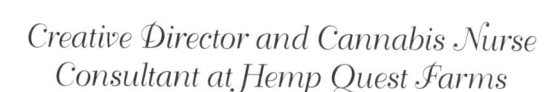

Creative Director and Cannabis Nurse Consultant at Hemp Quest Farms

Nicole Ryan, RN, CST, is an avid supporter of cannabinoid therapeutics. Upon graduating nursing school in 2019, she accepted a position on a cardiovascular intensive care unit. Her personal cannabis journey and her professional cannabis journey soon became intertwined. After exploring the emerging specialty of cannabis nursing, her determination to educate her clients with evidence-based science became her passion. Nicole joined Hemp Quest Farms in 2021 as a Cannabis Nurse Consultant. She considers herself a lifelong student and is currently enrolled in a college-level, accredited Medical Cannabis Certificate program. Nicole is also a proud member of the American Cannabis Nurses Association.

A Southeast Massachusetts native, Nicole now calls North Carolina home. She enjoys digging in her gardens, spending time with her rescue pup, and summertime traveling with her longtime boyfriend, his son, and her niece, Ava.

JULIE LINEBERGER

JULIE LINEBERGER

CONVERSATION WITH JULIE LINEBERGER

> Julie, you are the President of Wheel Pad L3C. Tell us about your business and the people you serve.

Julie Lineberger: Wheel Pad provides Personal Accessible Dwellings (PADs) for people to live, work, and play where they want to. We believe in a very inclusive world where people with spinal cord injuries, or other mobility issues, should live how and where they want. We provide a variety of models that are built in factories and delivered across the country. Our most popular model is called an "+Add PAD." We take it to someone's house, work with their builder/contractor to create a five-foot connector, and within two weeks, a family can have an accessible bedroom and bathroom that connects to their home through a back door or window. Caregivers can enter the PAD via a ramp without going through the entire house. It is very exciting.

LEADING PROFESSIONALS AND BUSINESS OWNERS

Our Godson started living with quadriplegia shortly before his 26th birthday due to an accident. After rehabilitation, he moved to a new town to start a new job. Looking for an accessible place to rent, he couldn't find one where a caregiver could help him in the shower in Portland, Oregon, of all places. He was forced to live in an accessible hotel room for nine months before finally finding a rental.

Exhausted with a new job, new mobility situation, etcetera, he was unable to avail himself of offers from others to go out for a meal or other social activities. Living in a small hotel space, others could not cook for him there. He was very isolated.

Eventually, he purchased a home and called us, his Godparents, as our first business is LineSync Architecture. He said, "Hey, I bought this house. Can you help me make it universally accessible?" There is a Vimeo of our work with him: Universal Design on a Budget: (https://vimeo.com/112705129)

During that process, my husband, who is an inventive type, mused, "What if there had been an accessible bedroom and bathroom that we could have attached to your mom's house or your brother's house, so you wouldn't have been isolated in an accessible motel room while you searched for an accessible rental?" That's where the idea of +Add PAD surfaced.

> **Can you give us more details about Wheel Pad models and the available options?**

Julie Lineberger: PADs are specifically built for people with mobility issues, although anyone can live in them, thus the term Universal Design. Each PAD has an installed ceiling hoist track, for example. Everything is made to exceed ADA standards and AARP Guidelines. We initially marketed to people with spinal cord injuries. Yet, with Covid, we've had numerous people call to ask: "How quickly can you get an +Add PAD to my house so I can get my mother out of the nursing home?" Depending on each town's permitting issues, we can make that happen within a couple of weeks. +Add PAD is 200 square feet and contains an accessible bedroom and bathroom. Because it was created with our then 26-year-old Godson, who is very design-oriented in mind, we like to say, "It's the coolest room in the house." It doesn't look like a hospital room. It looks like a room that you would want to hang out in all the time.

Through the connector, one can roll in for family dinners and activities, retreating as we all do to a private space. PADs are built with highly insulated panels for comfort in colder climates which also provides sound insulation.

One customer was a Vietnam veteran. The Veterans Affairs provides Specially Adapted Housing grants to cover the cost of accessibility modifications. Wheel Pad L3C is an approved contractor for this program. He was living with ALS and slowly losing mobility in his legs. He really liked +Add PAD in concept, yet he still wanted to sleep next to his wife. +Add PAD has room for either a hospital bed or a double bed, not the queen size he desired. Thus we created XL PAD!

+Add PADs are built on a chassis so that any veteran with a friend with an F350 truck or equivalent can come to pick it up and truck it home. XL PAD has all the same amenities, such as the hoist track and the accessible wet room shower, and it fits a queen-sized bed. The main difference is the necessity to be delivered on a flatbed and lifted into place with a crane. For the duration of his life, this man was able to sleep next to his wife, for which he and his wife were grateful. About nine months after he passed away, I asked his wife about her interest in re-selling the XL PAD as we have a resale program that we offer to our customers. She liked XL PAD so much; she was insistent upon keeping it. She said she loved the natural light in XL PAD, and that was where she felt close to her husband. XL PAD is now her bedroom, leaving the house bedrooms for family and guests.

"Mi PAD" is our newest model. As far as we can see, Mi PAD is the first accessible tiny house. With most tiny houses, the sleeping area is in a loft, not practical for one with mobility issues. We are starting to roll this model out now, including all of the same signature features as our other PADs.

LineSync Architecture is a registered B Corporation that mandates rigorous standards for energy efficiency and other sustainability features and transparent business practices. Thus, when designing PADs for Wheel Pad, standard features include specifications for highly insulated walls, ceiling, floor, and windows. Energy-efficient heating and cooling and non-toxic materials contribute to the quality of the product and are placed to enhance the beauty of the design in general. All +Add PADs can be reused through our guaranteed buyback program!

> **Do you serve clients across the country?**

Julie Lineberger: Yes, we do. We currently have manufacturers in Vermont, Massachusetts, and Texas. We are about to add another one in Oregon. We don't charge for delivery. Our mission is to keep families together. We often hear of injured service members at Walter Reed, other VA facilities, or nursing homes isolated from their families simply because they don't have accessible homes.

We want families to be together, and we have been able to make that happen. Since we want to help as many people as possible, we incorporated it as an L3C, a low-profit limited liability company. It's a hybrid between a for-profit and a non-profit. We're working diligently to keep costs as affordable as possible for as many people as possible while paying our manufacturers fairly and paying our staff living wages.

> **Before the Wheel Pad option, what were people doing? What other options did they have?**

Julie Lineberger: That is the best question ever. Thank you for asking. People are spending 6 to 9 months hiring contractors, designers, architects, and builders to put additions on their homes. That takes a lot of time and a lot of decision-making. When dealing with a recent spinal cord injury or someone in a nursing home, especially during COVID-19, both the injured and the family just want the loved one out of an institution and back to a family situation. Even modifying a bedroom or bathroom can be time-consuming, stressful, and expensive. We make it as easy as possible.

Unfortunately, the other alternatives include loved ones being stuck in nursing homes and rehab facilities only because their homes aren't accessible. People also bring a hospital bed into their living room, wreaking havoc on marriage and family. People with mobility issues don't want to feel like they are disrupting the entire family. They deserve a place of their own that is comfortable and private, where they can maintain their dignity. It is estimated only 7% of families who need accessibility actually have accessible homes. The rest are making do in unimaginable ways.

> **What inspired you to create Wheel Pad?**

Julie Lineberger: As I mentioned previously, our first business is LineSync Architecture. We, as individuals and as a business, are very inclusive. It's important for us to have diversity in our business and our general thinking. Diversity of thought makes our designs better, and we've had several people with varying abilities work for us. We have done many ADA jobs, such as redoing courthouses and other public buildings to meet ADA standards. All of our works use concepts of Universal Designs from the initial concept stage, integrating the thought process into every aspect of a home, corporate headquarters, or public building, such as a recent design for the Carinthia Base Lodge at Mount Snow. Many do not think accessibility might be significant at a ski lodge; however, the rise in Adaptive Sports is phenomenal!!!

Our Godson, Riley, has been an inspiration for us. He came to his home mountain for the X Games. At the time, he was a hotshot photographer doing a documentary on Simon Dumont, who won the X Games that year. There was a big celebration, and an accident occurred with Riley in the pool. To this day, only the people there know what happened. It left Riley with minimal movement in his body. Since then, he has worked very hard and made significant improvements. We have been honored to help keep Riley's spirits up and make his first home universally accessible. My husband would always talk about how nice it would be to have a pre-made, accessible addition so that it could be all ready for Riley when he came home from rehab. We all loved the idea. We sat around on it for about five years, and one day my friend said, "Julie, you really need to make a go of this. I am hosting a business plan competition, and I think you should throw your hat in the ring." Being on the "other side of 50," I was hesitant to start a new business venture. It has all been worth it. We have achieved our goal of keeping families together, and everyone we have worked with has been so grateful and appreciative. It's just fantastic.

I have to tell you one more story about Riley. During his recovery, he was working with an acupuncturist that came to his home. After about nine months, she told Riley, "I'm sorry, but I can't be your physician anymore." Riley was devastated, as he had fallen head over heels in love with the doctor but would never say anything because he valued her being a part of his health journey. At his look, she continued: "I've fallen in love with you." So here we are, a few years later, and they are a happy couple. They started a business together called "Poor House Love Lab," where they talk about what it is like to be an interabled couple. There are numerous interabled couples worldwide, especially in the United States, where there is more openness around accessibility and significant medical advances. Andrea and Riley are amazing as individuals and as a couple.

> For people who would like to know more about Wheel Pad L3C and the freedom it can offer their families, how do they find you and connect with you?

Julie Lineberger: Our website is www.wheelpad.com. You can also find us on YouTube, Facebook, Linked In, and Twitter. If you check out "TEDx Hoboken: Wheel Pad Keeping Families Together" on YouTube, it gives a great sense of the Wheel Pad origin story and people we have assisted simply by doing what we enjoy doing. If anyone would like to speak to me directly, send an email to julie@wheelpad.com.

JULIE LINEBERGER

President, Wheel Pad L3C

Julie Lineberger, EdM Harvard, is a successful entrepreneur and President of Wheel Pad L3C, providing accessible living and working spaces for people with mobility challenges, keeping families together in emergency, temporary, or permanent situations. Offerings include accessible bed/bath additions, accessible tiny homes, accessible workspaces, and accessible multi-unit buildings. All PADs are built with standard features

LEADING PROFESSIONALS AND BUSINESS OWNERS

to make it easier to live, play, and work from the comfort of one's own home.

Her past success with LineSync Architecture, a green and sustainable firm in southern Vermont, garnered numerous awards for both Design and Business Management. A previous career in International Development included managing and participating in projects for the United Nations Development Program, the International Rescue Committee, and the United Nations High Commissioner for Refugees throughout the world.

As current chair of Green America Board of Directors and past chair of Vermont Businesses for Social Responsibility Board of Directors, Julie leads many workshops and is a consultant on various aspects of business management. She is also involved in various community efforts and maintains positive, healthy work environments at LineSync Architecture and Wheel Pad L3C.

WEBSITE:
www.wheelpad.com

EMAIL:
julie@wheelpad.com

FACEBOOK:
https://www.facebook.com/wheelpad

LINKEDIN:
https://www.linkedin.com/company/10576355/

MECHELLE TUCKER

MECHELLE TUCKER

CONVERSATION WITH MECHELLE TUCKER

> **Mechelle, you are the Founder of 1st Class Consultant, a digital consulting agency based in Arizona. Tell us about your agency and the people that you serve.**

Mechelle Tucker: 1st Class Consultant was established in 2008. Entrepreneurs and business owners need support and leadership. They need mentors, advisors, and consultants whom they can trust to give them solid information and steer them in the right direction. I felt a huge void in the marketplace for this kind of service, as I was also an entrepreneur with limited support. It was very lonely trying to navigate without help, resources, or funding to make what I refer to as "win-win-wins" happen. I wanted to be part of the solution since I knew what it felt like to have that problem. I support entrepreneurs from various industries, including entertainment, technology, cannabis, and fashion, to name a few. I have been blessed to work with so many unique business owners, helping them make "win-win-wins" happen.

> **What are the most common challenges and voids that business owners face?**

Mechelle Tucker: I feel many of them are lacking inspiration, encouragement, and support. Sometimes all it takes is one call, one quote, one text, one person to lean on that says, "Hey, you've got this, you're going to be okay." I can give them a third-party viewpoint to help assess their situation. Sometimes you become so consumed with being an entrepreneur, hustling every single day, that you don't get to stop and smell the roses and realize you have made significant accomplishments, developed assets, and ROIs. Small business owners don't have the staff as large corporations do. They need the right leadership and support in their corner.

> Business owners often are great at their craft but don't realize that it takes more than that. You have to advertise, market, and create a presence on social media. Do the business owners that you help realize when they lack these things? Or do you have to create awareness?

Mechelle Tucker: A little bit of both. I'm really big on mindset; a healthy, positive mindset matters. People just kind of get caught up in the day-to-day of it. It's like being on a rollercoaster ride. Entrepreneurs have their highs and lows. So you just have to buckle your seatbelt and go with it. For me, it has been all about understanding my "why." I've been through so many experiences that could have caused me just to give up. But I never forget my "why," and that consistency is key. If you keep building and have passion for what you do, they will come. It shouldn't even feel like work. I help my clients be passion-driven and make sure there is an emotional connection to what they are doing. When they have that friendly, 1st Class Consulting reminder, it keeps them focused on their "why."

> **Can you tell us a story about a game-changing moment in your business?**

Mechelle Tucker: Two years ago, I had the opportunity to go to Kampala, Uganda, to assist clients abroad. It was my first time traveling outside of the United States. From a business standpoint, there were many challenges from the moment I stepped off the plane. However, on the fifth day of my visit, I was seated at the President of Kampala's table. I attribute this to being a good listener, having a keen ability to understand others, and implementing strategies in a less than ideal situation. I overcame the hurdle of being in another country and powered forward to help yet another client gain clarity about their business.

> **What inspired you to get into the field of business consulting?**

Mechelle Tucker: I've always had the "gift of gab." Since the beginning of my career, I have worked in sales and marketing and been a pillar in my community, network, and family. I'm an excellent giver. But sometimes I'm not the best receiver. So I was honored for your team to find me and spotlight me in this book, which made me realize the value I offer had spoken for itself. Like I mentioned earlier, you have to smell the roses sometimes. We get so caught up in the grind that we forget where we came from. I have done this for almost 12 years, and it hasn't always been easy. But I have the tenacity, and I never forget my "why." My time and freedom mean a lot to me. I have been a wife for 20 years, and I have children ranging from 5 to 27. Being an entrepreneur was necessary for me to still dedicate time to being a wife, mom and have the quality of life I wanted for my family. But in that journey, we all need the right leadership, mentors, supporters, and advisors to inspire us along the way. I've been honored to be that vessel in business, to be the light in times of darkness for other entrepreneurs. I'm so grateful that God blessed me to have the energy, tenacity, love, and compassion to see all business owners win. This is my goal and my dream.

> **For business owners that resonate with your message and your passion, how can they find you and connect with you?**

Mechelle Tucker: My website is www.1stclassconsultant.com. Outside of that, I am on every social media platform you can imagine. You can connect with me on LinkedIn or Instagram @michellesecrets. I have a club on the new app called "Clubhouse." We're hosting events there, and our goal is to align ourselves with like-minded, like-hearted, and like-spirited people. We drop gems, tips, business resources, and business blessings. Sometimes we do pop-up events just to bless a business owner in need financially. I am striving to branch out more into the philanthropy and humanitarian components because there is no goodwill or SOS for business owners. If you lack resources or funding, where do you turn for help? I want to be part of that solution, making sure business owners have their basic needs met.

MECHELLE TUCKER

Founder, 1st Class Consultant

Mechelle Cherie Tucker is "The Networkers Networker." She is an extraordinary businesswoman and networker. Mechelle comes to light as a consultant and entrepreneur with tenacity and prowess to transform businesses and business owners into front runners. Mechelle is devoted to bringing quality, practical, and personalized consultancy services to your table. With over a decade of experience as a global consultant, she is widely respected for her talent and ability to resolve critical issues knowledgeably and expeditiously. She is the founder of 1st Class Consultant, LLC., a consultancy firm dedicated to providing valuable top-notch services that help companies and various business firms achieve their desired goals through professional consultancy, creative marketing, and management services. She can also be defined by her hunger to motivate people and inspire change in their businesses.

Having worked within several facets of her field, she desired to be dynamic in her services to people. She recognized the need for change, seeking a more refined approach in an ever-evolving, globalized, and digitalized business world. In search of such uniqueness, she has continuously expanded her knowledge base, keeping abreast of trends in the business world to remain relevant in the field. Mechelle is a valuable asset to industries, businesses, and organizations, regardless of their niche. With diverse skills to function in several aspects of business and a strong desire to touch people's lives positively, she has hosted, organized, and managed hundreds of events nationally with the presence of reputable personalities and celebrities.

"1st Class Consultant is my experience developed into a brand with a team of strategists and independent contractors behind us. We are here to help our clients understand how marketing, events, and branding services can increase business. 1st Class Consulting services are about teaching, showing, and then doing," said Mechelle Tucker. Mechelle is committed to quality service delivery that yields incredible results. She remains a devoted wife and a wonderful mother that is dedicated, hardworking, creative, and successful.

BUSINESS BIO:

1st Class Consultant is a creative services firm developed to elevate client visibility and strategize effective brand management. 1st Class Consultant engages in all types of business mediums and is perfectly aware of the trending market changes. All of this makes 1st Class one of the best consultancy firms, representing sizeable incomes for all clients. 1st Class Consultant has vast experience working on events related to the Grammy's, NBA All-Star, WNBA All-Star, BET Awards, AZ Pro Bowl Weekend, NFL Super Bowl Weekend, The Million Dollar Mingle, The Celebrity Mama's Brunch, The Hollywood Charity Mixer, and Mechelle Secrets Hennessy X.O Trailblazer Toast to name a few. 1st Class Consultant lists a variety of clients and a CV work portfolio on its website. 1st Class Consultant, LLC Firm provides our clients, sponsors, partners, contractors, collaborators, and vendors with tangible business solutions to their problems. It helps them overcome weaknesses and directs them on a path of desired outcomes through our professional consultancy, marketing, or management services. 1st Class Consultant has commandeered hundreds of successful independent, corporate, and celebrity events providing exceptional services that redefine a new wave of creating Win-Win-Wins in business. 1st Class Consultant has been featured on numerous radio shows and

LEADING PROFESSIONALS AND BUSINESS OWNERS

news publications to share insight on philanthropy, business, social media, networking, and current events.

WEBSITE:
www.1stclassconsultant.com | www.1stclassnotary.com | www.twisttoaxis.com

INSTAGRAM:
@mechellesecrets

TWITTERL:
@mechelle1st

CLUBHOUSE:
@mechellesecrets

FACEBOOK:
@1stclassconsultant

TIK TOK:
@mechellesecrets

LINKEDIN:
@mechelletucker

EMAIL:
Mechelle@1stclassconsultant.com

BUSINESS PHONE:
623.349.1146

KAREN YEE

KAREN YEE
CONVERSATION WITH KAREN YEE

> Karen, you are a sales coach out of New York City and the founder of New Futures On Demand. Tell us about your business and the type of people you help.

Karen Yee: I genuinely believe that everyone has a skill set that they're passionate about and that they can create a profitable business, especially during this Pandemic, a profitable online business. I started at the typical 8:00 to 5:00 corporate job, and after a while, I just wasn't passionate about what I was doing anymore. I am passionate about marketing and sales and helping other entrepreneurs. So I started my company to help small and medium-sized business owners learn how to position themselves to be more visible and scale using ads. I realized this isn't something taught in universities or colleges because when you get your degree, you are thrown out into the real world, where you are really good at what you do, but when it comes to marketing, it is an entirely new language. Many people are not very comfortable with it. I provide my clients with the knowledge and tools they can grasp, which turns into an asset that they can put in their asset column so that anything they do for their business is not a liability.

> **What is positioning, and why is it essential in the marketing world?**

Karen Yee: Positioning is how you describe what you do to your audiences on the platform or platforms you are on, whether it be Facebook, Instagram, LinkedIn, or Twitter. If someone is interested in learning more about you and seeing if you can help them, there are many ways that person can find you. Let's take Facebook, for example. If this person lands on your Facebook page and sees that all you talk about is how you love puppies and on other platforms you're professional, this person will be confused about what you actually do. It is beneficial to position yourself in the same way across all social media platforms to be seen and known as the expert in your field.

> **Once someone has their positioning and messages in place, how do they get people to connect with them?**

Karen Yee: There is a strategy that I teach my clients. Many people are uncomfortable posting and neglect the platforms they are on. The strategy I teach gets people to become more engaged as they learn about and trust you. Additionally, I also teach content strategy and precisely what to post to help your sales process and take people through the customer journey from start to finish.

> **What is the most common challenge your clients face?**

Karen Yee: The mindset around marketing and sales aspects. Generally, the clients I work with have some leads but struggle with the marketing and sales side to get more. Many people simply aren't comfortable. I always say this "be comfortable with being uncomfortable." To be an entrepreneur, you have to be comfortable being uncomfortable and putting yourself out there. You've already taken the first risky step of becoming your own boss. Now all you need to do is take the next logical steps to "next level" yourself, and I help people get through those mental blocks and limitations to get there.

> **What does it take to be successful in sales? What do you teach?**

Karen Yee: Think about the sales process like you are talking to a friend. There is a misconception about sales because people think they have to sound like a car salesperson. Think of it as solving a problem for your client. Let's say you have low back pain. You go to the doctor because you want to be diagnosed. The doctor performs an exam and gives you a prescription, whether it be an MRI, X-ray, or medication. And most people don't think of it this way, but that doctor is actually selling you a prescription or a solution to your problem. Look at it the same way when it comes to your own business. It takes the pressure off selling when you look at it as diagnosing a problem and providing a prescription.

What inspired you to start New Futures On Demand?

Karen Yee: I came from the corporate world, and we worked with a lot of entrepreneurs who needed capital funding. When it came to the marketing and selling aspects, I saw firsthand how much people struggled. I started my company to bridge that gap, hence the name "New Futures On Demand." This program is also for people who are currently in the corporate 9:00 to 5:00 grind and are thinking about transitioning out to start their own business. You truly can create a business where you wake up in the morning and are super excited about what you do, a business you are passionate about and successful in. The best time for you to take advantage of this was yesterday. The second best time is now today.

> How can people that would benefit from your sales coaching find you and connect with you?

Karen Yee: Definitely reach out and don't be scared. You deserve to do well. Find me on Facebook at Karen Yee or Instagram at kare_yee. You can also email me at hello@newfuturesondemand.com.

KAREN YEE

Sales Coach
Founder of New Futures On Demand

Karen Yee is the Founder of New Futures On Demand and a believer that everyone has the ability to create a new future with their skillset. She guides small to medium companies and individuals to build a winning profile and quantum leap their business profitably and predictably. Learn how to make that money work hard for you.

LEADING PROFESSIONALS AND BUSINESS OWNERS

Karen created the Art of Selling Mastermind™, an online training program that helps people uncover, brand, package, and sell their services, so they create more impact and build their "work from anywhere" dream lifestyle. Karen has been an online marketer in New York for almost ten years and helped professional brands earn collectively millions of dollars by building their online business.

WEBSITE:
newfuturesondemand.com

EMAIL:
hello@newfuturesondemand.com

FACEBOOK:
https://www.facebook.com/karen.yee.3958

INSTAGRAM:
https://www.instagram.com/kare_yee

GEORGE DANDRIDGE JR.

GEORGE DANDRIDGE JR.

CONVERSATION WITH GEORGE DANDRIDGE JR.

> George, you are the Founder and President of Dandridge Investment Group in Dallas, Texas. Tell us about Dandridge Investment Group and the people you help.

George Dandridge Jr: Dandridge Investment Group was initially founded as Elite 8 Tax and Financial Services back in 2013. Currently, it parents the companies Elite 8 Tax and Financial Services (the flagship brand offering premium tax services and generational wealth-building tools), Elite 8 Tax Pro (which focuses on training and supporting new tax professionals), BOSS (an acronym for Business Operations Success Strategies), and BOSS talk radio, which is a weekly program with several different segments where we highlight business owners and their plights in business. I believe small business drives the economy. I'm committed to providing the tools essential for small business operations to keep them going and position them for success.

> **What is a common challenge that entrepreneurs face today?**

George Dandridge Jr: Many entrepreneurs hit an absolute dark space where they have to decide whether to continue or quit. We never hear the stories of those who choose to quit. The ones who double down in that space and persevere with tenacity, risking family, finances, and stability, are the ones who have the breakthrough. Everyone wants to do business with someone who is committed.

Another common problem is people don't put enough planning or thought into their business. Maybe they haven't written out a business plan or have one that is outdated. And just because you plan for a sunny picnic, it doesn't mean there aren't going to be some clouds you have to prepare for. The clouds bring people to those common questions, "Do I keep going? Do I quit? I didn't plan for this." There is something to be said for having contingent strategies and building a team early. I can't tell you how many times I have heard business owners say, "Once I start making some profit, I'll hire an accountant." The reality is, if you hire an accountant early, you will ultimately save money and turn a profit so much sooner.

> **When business owners reach the point of continuing or quitting, are they thinking about getting a different job entirely?**

George Dandridge Jr: Often, it's either that or quitting a particular niche. One of the things I found is that overnight success usually takes about ten years or longer at the minimum. A social media narrative exists that tells us we will see success in a few months to a year, and most people are only built to endure two years of discomfort. It makes it very challenging for them to have a second year where they are getting even more responsibility or going more into debt as they are trying to grow. But it takes time for people to know, like, and trust you, or even just be aware of you. When the fallacy of family and friends supporting the business owner doesn't work out, they find themselves without a follow-up plan. People often think that their sphere of influence or their perceived sphere of influence will contribute to their success. In actuality, these people don't know you, and you haven't earned their trust of doing business with you quite yet. And if you quit in a year or two, they will never get that chance.

Just recently, someone reached out to me on social media. I had sent her a message back in 2014 soliciting the opportunity to earn her business through a referral program. I had only been in business for a year at that point. And here we were just a couple of weeks ago; this person reached out to me because she saw a post I made about helping people with tax problems. She had to laugh at herself because she had let her tax problems snowball, as people typically do to avoid dealing with them. My post spoke to her in a very caring way, and she remembered that I had reached out to her six or seven years prior. So you have to remain consistent and always improve to become an authority in your space. Too often, we get comfortable too quickly: "If you build it, they will come." Some people really believe that once they hang the sign, they will be a millionaire tomorrow. It doesn't work that way.

> **As well as helping people with tax problems, beyond that, you help people overcome challenges with their business. You "meet them where they're at," so to speak. At the end of the day, they get to know, like, and trust you for your expertise in other areas, and then say, "Oh, by the way. I have a tax problem." Is that what brings them to you?**

George Dandridge Jr: You know, that part for me is the passion part; the absolute impact part. It's the part of me that speaks to the child that had these feelings of wanting to be an entrepreneur but lacked the guidance and direction of how to sustain. My passion is to help as many people as possible avoid failures. This is how BOSS (Business Operations Success Strategies) came to be. It's currently a book that I'm working on that will be released later this year. Those services include payroll, bookkeeping, entity formation, tax planning and compliance, and all of these intricate things that people don't really consider. Hopefully, I can keep my clients on the BOSS side of the tax resolution piece because it is more fun and less expensive here. Don't get me wrong, I enjoy fighting with the government for you, but things are much more intricate and expensive over there. So the operational part of my business is passion because I had to learn to embrace this gift I was given. When I would go out with a group of friends, and they were enamored with the ambiance of a restaurant, I was sitting there calculating how much money they were taking in. I've always been "that guy."

> **What inspired you to get into the field of financial services and help people solve tax problems?**

George Dandridge Jr: It wasn't a single event; it was really more of a journey. I always had a sort of sick, twisted, "figure out the money" gift. But I'm also of the age where I was taught that you get a job, you work there for 40 years, and then you retire. But obviously, the landscape of the job market has changed. There was a time when I was an employee, and I had to chase the check. I was moving every two to three years wherever the company would send me. I also had a thing with authority, so I always had a second or a third job because

LEADING PROFESSIONALS AND BUSINESS OWNERS

I wanted the freedom to brush someone off if I needed to. I would never compromise myself for a check.

In 2012, I was getting ready to travel to Hawaii. I had a nasty habit of smoking cigarettes at that time. I heard everything in Hawaii was super expensive. I was going to buy a carton of cigarettes before I left, and my debit card was declined. This was infuriating and scary all at the same time. I had no idea what was going on. So like anyone who knows they have money in the bank, I asked them to rerun it. We repeated that process two times. I came to find out that the IRS had put a lien on my account. I was in an absolute panic. I didn't have credit cards, only my bank account. And I was set to leave for Hawaii in less than 24 hours for ten days with other people that were depending on me. I knew a woman who worked in the tax industry as an enrolled agent, and I called her to see if she could help me. She had me send some stuff over to her, and by the time I landed in Hawaii, I had full access to my bank account. It blew me away! At that point, I really wanted to learn more about what she did and how she did it.

The other part was just really feeling burned out on the corporate scene. It was frustrating trying to figure out how to climb the ladder; I've never been good at politics. I was tired of it after 14 years. I relocated to Dallas, and for the first time in my life, I had a difficult time finding a career opportunity that would pay me what I was used to making. This went on for about six months until I decided to try my hand in the tax industry. I was already interested in it and had been spending time studying it. I got addicted so quickly. I would read tax code like people watch reality TV. The more I would read, the more intoxicated I became. I started to expand my professional circle as it related to colleagues in the industry and learned more about niche markets and specializations I would be able to travel in upon receiving certain designations. I just smashed down on the gas pedal and doubled down.

On a side note, I did end up finding out why the IRS put that lien on my account. Many years prior, I filed my taxes after Hurricane Katrina. My original tax professional was not in business anymore, so I had to choose someone new. I received a large refund and thought it was due to damages to my house from Katrina and things of that nature. Well, it turns out that you can be audited on nothing other than who your tax professional is. If they have many irregularities, the IRS will choose to audit anything with their numbers assigned to it. I got caught up in something that went on for years and ultimately ended with me not having access to my money. But if it weren't for that experience, I wouldn't have found my passion for the tax code.

> **What advice would you give to people on the fence about starting their own business or even considering leaving the business they are in?**

George Dandridge Jr: There's no cookie-cutter response for that because the individual actually matters. Everyone is not built with the same degree of fortitude, nor do they have the same objectives. But it is absolutely imperative for everyone to know and fully understand their "why." Otherwise, you will not be able to face the challenges you are presented with. When asked that question, most people will say their "why" is their kids or some level of financial success, but it has to be *more* than that. One of the things that people reading this may pick up on is my absolute excitement when I start to talk about business operations and tax matters and things of that nature. And the thing is, I was blessed to be able to discover those passions. So I fully understood my "why" going in. I want to be that person someone can call to immediately have the IRS back off because my teaching and business operations kick in, and it hits on all cylinders. I will not allow anyone to believe that there are no downsides to business, despite all of the success that I have experienced. There are daily operational things that I am in the process of building teams for because I just don't want to do it anymore. I want more time to focus on the passion part. But there are some essential screws that you have to tighten here and there and things you have to build. So you have to be along for the process. Progress is a process. Commitment is the elimination of all options. You have to understand those two things to have the fortitude to reach that ten year or beyond mark to have overnight success.

> **For people that could use your business or tax help, how can they find you and connect with you?**

George Dandridge Jr: On the tax side, you can reach us at 866-235-4838. Someone will answer your call, walk you through an interview process to determine what the problems are, create secure portals so we can exchange information, and take up your problem and your fight, so you don't have to. On the operations side, there are two parts. We have the radio show, and you can schedule to interview at sales@talkbossradio.com. If you are looking for any services or coaching, we also offer a virtual CFO service. You can find those services at Elite8financial.com/boss. When you go there, you'll see everything from entity setup, payroll, bookkeeping, life insurance, or anything else you can think of from a financial or compliance aspect to support small businesses.

GEORGE DANDRIDGE JR.

Founder and President
Dandridge Investment Group / Elite 8 Tax & Financial Services

George Dandridge is a New Orleans native, military veteran, business executive, seasoned tax professional, and serial entrepreneur. His passions lie in business, community, family, and music. His approach to business, life, and obstacles, in general, is the simple question, "What's the Objective?" George feels that this approach prevents one from getting boxed into limited or traditional thinking.

George Dandridge Jr. is an Enrolled Agent, Founder and President of Dandridge Investment Group, which parents Elite 8 Tax and Financial Services and Elite Tax Pro Solutions. He's also a board and founding member of the National Association of Black Tax Professionals and the host of BOSS Talk Radio.

George Dandridge formed 8th Wonder Enterprises, later named Dandridge Investment Group, in 2007 and has found success in entertainment, restaurants, and business management. Since 2013 he has been successful in the tax industry as a go-to company for tax solutions.

WEBSITE:
Elite8financial.com/boss

EMAIL:
sales@talkbossradio.com

PHONE:
866-235-4838

CAM CALLENDER

CAM CALLENDER

CONVERSATION WITH CAM CALLENDER

> Cam, you are the Founder of MSI Mind. Tell us about your business and the people you serve.

Cam Callender: The MSI concept is an income stream segment based on the different types of income streams. I have narrowed them down to eight specific types. Those different types are independent of each other, but they also can complement each other, and you can build from one stream to the next. I consult with people showing them how to take one income stream and build it into another type, rather than thinking about two jobs as two income streams. As we've seen with COVID, jobs can easily change. Having different income streams can build a safety net for you, as long as they are independent of each other. Some of them are passive, while others are direct sales. If you have a job, you can have something else on the side, such as an eBay or Etsy store where you profit from sales. You can also start to build investments that give you a return. So some are passive, and some require a little bit of work. But all in all, you can set them up to operate on their own.

> **What does your ideal client look like?**

Cam Callender: Most of the people I work with have an entrepreneurial spirit. They don't want just to work a job forever, and some realize they can't work a job forever. For example, construction workers or other people who do hard labor recognize that their bodies will break down eventually. Even if they love the job, they can't physically do it forever. So they want to develop something for themselves that will act as a safety net in the future, as far as income goes.

> **What are some common myths and misconceptions about multiple streams of income?**

Cam Callender: People often view multiple jobs as multiple streams of income. But if it is the same type, there are pitfalls. Jobs are just one stream, no matter how many you have. The key is to diversify your income types. For example, one type of income stream is stock portfolios. If you have one or two jobs, you also want to make sure you have investments and dividend income. Many people in the direct sales market think they have multiple income streams because they sell more than one product. But they are still in the same space with the same customer base. Even if they sold 15 different products, the same pitfalls could occur with each one. By having multiple income streams, if one slows down, the others can pick up the slack. I was working in the travel industry, and when travel slowed down due to COVID, my other income streams kicked in, and I was able to move forward with those.

> **What does the process look like when someone decides to work with you?**

Cam Callender: The income streams are ordered one through eight. The first thing I do is find out which income streams my client currently has to see the foundation we have to work from. From there, we develop a plan for where they want to go and what their goals are. Everyone has different goals and different numbers they want to reach regarding what they want out of life and their retirement.

> **What inspired you to become an entrepreneur?**

Cam Callender: For me, it began right at the dawn of the internet, back in the dial-up days. Once I was able to get online, I wanted to find ways to make money. When I was a kid, I came home from school and took surveys online to make money. I had my regular allowance from my parents, but I always had that itch to earn more so I could spend it on whatever I wanted. From there, I developed an eBay store and sold drop-ship items online, right when the internet started. Then I moved into direct sales and began selling Cutco knives. Direct sales strengthened my entrepreneurial drive, and I continued developing products, selling, and broadening my skill set. I knew it was something I could do, but I wanted to create concepts that other people could follow to have the lifestyles they always wanted. I continued to mold the concepts into something customizable for each unique client that I serve.

Was there a breakthrough moment for you?

Cam Callender: I used to have the same mindset I spoke of previously, thinking that multiple jobs were equivalent to multiple income streams. I worked very hard in network marketing, and my original MSI concept was to have multiple network marketing programs. I realized as the old saying goes, "Never put all your eggs in one basket." So I revamped and redeveloped the MSI concept into the eight income streams and have focused on those with my clients ever since.

> **What are some of the income streams that you teach?**

Cam Callender: I teach people how to invest in different ways. You can make stock investments, and I will show clients my dividend portfolio, which are stocks that are solely dividend-producing. You can have dividend income and stock income, including capital gains. I have also gotten into some IPOs and similar investments early on with websites like Wefunder, where you can begin investing in things you love. Another great income stream is rental income through owning properties. Real estate can be a passive income stream as you grow and get other people to manage the properties while still bringing in money.

> **Which income stream is your favorite?**

Cam Callender: Income stream #4 - Residual Income. We have residual bills, so we need to develop residual income to cover them.

> **When is the right time to look into the MSI Mind concept?**

Cam Callender: When you have realized that you want something more and are ready to diversify your portfolio. Many clients come to me after learning that their current career is not going to be the "end all, be all" for them. By starting to build other income streams now, they can eventually leave that position without hesitation. It will take some time to build those foundations, so the sooner you start, the better.

> **For people resonating with your message, how can they find you and connect with you?**

Cam Callender: My website is MSImind.com. You can also Google me by name: Cam Callender. Feel free to contact me through my social media profiles. They are all public, and you can send me a message anytime to find out more.

CAM CALLENDER

Founder of MSI Mind

Cam Callender is always here to help and will never quit! He is a well of knowledge through experience. He only shares products he has personally used to share with you firsthand his own experience with each product or service he represents. His Information Technology background has Cam well-versed in technology and the use of many technology platforms and applications. This well-versed experience allows Cam to help many people in multiple ways in different situations. It is the MSIMIND way to bring critical thinking to situations to solve problems with multiple solutions.

Cam Callender is a Master Strategist in life and can help you brainstorm new solutions. There are multiple paths to reach the same end goal, so if you have a goal, Cam is one to help you reach that goal while trying to identify the most efficient path to completion. Any goal will be approached objectively without judgment with the MSI Concept.

WEBSITE:
msimind.com

EMAIL:
camcallender@msimind.com

FACEBOOK:
fb.com/camcal85

INSTAGRAM:
Instagram.com/camcallender

LINKEDIN:
https://www.linkedin.com/in/camcal85

YOUTUBE:
camcallender.org

DIANE STRAND

DIANE STRAND

CONVERSATION WITH DIANE STRAND

> Diane, you are the Founder of JDS Video and Media Productions, JDS Actors Studio, and the nonprofit JDS Creative Academy. Tell us about JDS and the people you help.

Diane Strand: We're all about visual, performing, and digital arts. JDS is a multi-award-winning production company for marketing and corporate communications, creating website videos and "how-tos." We work with many prominent clients in the business and biotech industries. JDS is located in Temecula, California, and we work closely with our city, region, county, and local area chambers. Our Actor's Studio has launched over 100 actors into the entertainment industry. I was a producer in the entertainment industry, and I've been an entrepreneur for 17 years. Ten years ago, we, my partner in business and life, Scott Strand, launched the Actor's Studio out of the video production company. We have acting classes for youth, teens, and adults, and we have an industry workshop where we set them up with Hollywood agents to help them launch their acting careers. My husband and I co-founded the nonprofit JDS Creative Academy seven years ago, which provides education and hands-on training in the visual, performing, and digital arts. My passion is video production and workforce development, so our training programs focus on these areas, training video production skills and providing career pathway opportunities.

We also have K-12 classes that meet the California Education Code requirements for visual and performing arts, VAPA, whether that education is acting, musical theater, photography, scriptwriting, or fashion design. In addition, we have a program for adults with autism and developmental disabilities that teaches video production. We do that through a broadcast television show I executive produce called the "Spirit of Innovation," a local Riverside County, California magazine-style news and information program impacting 2.4 million people. The adults in the program help us in content development. They also have their own weekly micro TV news show called the "SOI Update." For the past year, they have provided news and information content to the radio station 102.5 The Vine, where our participants work with our writers to produce the news content. Then they record it for airing seven days a week, three times a day.

We are super busy. My job right now is making people's dreams come true. One of our largest events is called DigiFest Temecula. It's in its 5th year, and it just keeps growing and growing. It is a three-day international film festival competition and a networking event and conference for industry students, amateurs, and professionals. The community is also very involved and intrigued. We bring Hollywood to Temecula! We also have three live theater productions a year, a Haunted Studio event in October, and a sold-out summer camp program.

> As we are coming out of this pandemic, what's happening in your industry? What are people reaching out to you for these days?

Diane Strand: A year ago, everyone thought video was important, and it was a "must-have" for websites, but with the pandemic, video is everyone's go-to….. everything has now moved into the digital world. We are doing more live events than ever before, but now in the virtual world. We have a 7,000 square foot full broadcast-ready TV studio with a 40-foot green screen. We produced a 300 person attendee function into a live interactive, engaging live stream event, created corporate tours for clients and vendors of manufacturing lines in the biotech community, and did virtual graduation and retirement events along with preparing video messages for our local school districts to communicate with their communities. Everything is very technical, so we have to stay on top of the technical needs, increase our production capacity, and incorporate it into our training. Another program we have is a California State apprenticeship program, making sure the next generation is ready to come up behind us and have a pathway in a subjective industry. It is our goal at JDS to remove barriers for anyone who wants to work in this industry. Video Production, journalism, creativing; it's a grind, but very rewarding and exciting - you have to be ready to work and work hard, bring your passion, and collaborate.

What inspired you to create JDS?

Diane Strand: My career journey has been long, leading me to the launch of JDS; I started in this business as an actor, doing some commercials and lots of theater. One of my first entrepreneurial endeavors was running a children's theater in Hollywood, where adult actors would perform for bussed in schools on a field trip, exposing them to the arts culture. I found myself enjoying the producing, the directing, and the writing more than the acting, and I quickly realized I belonged behind the scenes. When I graduated college with a degree in radio, television, and film, I started writing and producing for the Disney Channel launching playhouse Disney, working for Universal Creative, Warner Bros and on shows such as ABC's "General Hospital," Bright Kauffman Crane's "Friends," and "Veronica's Closet." I also worked in the high def control room at Staples Center live streaming national Laker's basketball to Japan and NHL's King's games, including producing the

2000 National Democratic Convention, and working for HBO and Pay Per View for the Eric Clapton Concert and Barbra Streisand Live at the Shrine. Then I did a stint in corporate video, and I loved it. You get put into a little box in the entertainment industry, and you work inside a designated area. When I moved into corporate video, I got to do everything from concept development to scriptwriting, production, and post-production. I got dragged back in slightly to the reality television craze. My husband was a professional actor who was also directing, and we decided that we wanted to do our own thing. We had a three-year-old at the time and took that leap into the entrepreneur world, hoping our parachutes would open. We quit our jobs and the six-figure incomes, sold our house, packed everything up, and moved from Los Angeles to North County, San Diego. I've settled in Temecula, but we were in the North County area for a little bit when we launched our business.

Today, I laugh and say, "I have my own mini Warner Brothers," when I refer to my 7,000 square foot studio. Not only are we "doing," but we teach. I'm out there doing what I love every single day. Last weekend, I was doing a video production of a live theater production of "James and the Giant Peach" since the city can't have audiences. I just put to bed a historical documentary for third-graders who can't take field trips to Temecula's historical Vail Ranch, one of our landmarks here in Temecula. So we are pivoting along with the pandemic situation. I am more creative in my day to day now than I was working on fictional television. When someone asks me today what I do for a living, I say, "I make dreams come true." I provide HOPE, defined as Help One Person Everyday. I do this by communicating someone's business message to help them grow their business. I do this by launching a young actor's career, providing them introductions to agents and managers, giving them training they can rely on to forward their career or a stage to perform on. And I also have 20 participants with autism and developmental disabilities in our video production training program 25 hours a week. The next step is placing them into jobs within the city of Temecula and businesses like Storm Stadium. These adults who once only had a dream of working in this industry now have the training and soft professional skills to go and live their dreams.

> **Tell us more from a teaching standpoint. When people reach out to you, what are their dreams? Where do they want to work? How do you prepare them?**

Diane Strand: I have to start by saying that I'm just one half. My husband is the other half; he is the teacher/coach, we say he is the Show, and I am the Business, and together we are ShowBusiness. We are both very creative. I am the implementer who produces and pulls it all together. But my husband is the instructor, and he's the one with the patience to work with all of the actors and program participants. He helps all ages, from youth through adults. There are no guarantees of making you a star, but we have definite connections and a solid reputation, along with a proven pathway into opportunities. If you learn from us, you will have a craft you can rely on. You can then mold that craft to work in front of a camera, be on a live stage, or become a public speaker. Most of our students come from a 50-mile radius of Temecula. We are about 70 miles south of LA, and I tell all of my students that they have to be willing to do what it takes and put in the travel time. We bring in agents, and they will choose 5 to 8 actors from each showcase to represent. Some of our actors are incredibly successful. Our most significant success has been Corinne Massiah. She started with us at age nine and is now in high school. She was on an ABC show for several years under contract, had many guest star roles, and was in a movie with Samuel L. Jackson. She has done very well and is currently on FOX's show 911, playing Angela Bassett's daughter.

We have many adults making a living through acting as well. Our special needs adults come to us after bouncing around after high school and really just want to get to work. So we help by giving them the skills they need and introducing them to people willing to take chances on them. I love workforce development because it comes with great incentives for the employer. Our special needs students are able to have a job coach, so the employer is confident they can perform the job well before they need to think about the cost to bring them on as a direct hire. It has been the most rewarding part of my job. Sure, I can run you through my resume of A list shows and all of the cool people I have met, but none of that compares to making someone's dreams come true, and I get paid to do that.

> **How can people find you, connect with you, and learn more?**

Diane Strand: I am all over social media and pretty easy to find. My personal account is "Diane Strand" on Facebook, Instagram, YouTube, and Twitter. You can also search the business profile pages of "JDS Video and Media Productions," "JDS Studios," "JDS Actors Studio," and "JDS Creative Academy." Our TV show is "Spirit of Innovation" and can be found at SOI_News on YouTube. Digifest Temecula takes place every April, and you can Google that for more information. I'd love to connect with you and share your dreams.

Diane Strand | Facebook
Diane Strand (@dianestrand) • Instagram photos and videos
Diane Strand | LinkedIn
(1) JDS Studios | Facebook
(1) JDS Video & Media Productions, Inc. | Facebook
(1) JDS Actors Studio | Facebook
(1) JDS Creative Academy | Facebook
(1) Spirit of Innovation | Facebook

(1) DigiFest Temecula | Facebook
(19) Diane Strand (@JDSProductions) / Twitter
JDS Creative Academy (@JDSCreative) / Twitter
JDS Actors Studio (@JDSActorsStudio) / Twitter
Spirit of Innovation (@SOI_newsinfo) / Twitter
DigiFest Temecula 2021 (@DigifestTemecu) / Twitter
JDSProductionStudios (@jdsproductionstudios) • Instagram photos and videos
JDS Actors Studio (@jdsactorsstudio) • Instagram photos and videos
JDS Creative Academy (@jdscreativeacademy) • Instagram photos and videos
Spirit of Innovation (@soi_newsinfo) • Instagram photos and videos
Digifest Temecula (@digifesttemecula) • Instagram photos and videos
www.jds-productions.com
www.jdsactorsstudio.com
www.jdscreativeacademy.org
www.jdsstudios.live

JDS Studio
28069 Diaz Rd. Ste D. E, F
Temecula, CA 92590
951-296-6715

DIANE STRAND

Founder of JDS Video and Media Productions, JDS Actors Studio, and Nonprofit JDS Creative Academy

Diane Strand is the majority owner and executive producer of the multi-award-winning JDS Video & Media Productions, Inc., the studio producer at JDS Actors Studio, and the founder and executive director of the nonprofit 501c3 JDS Creative Academy. She is also the creator and executive producer of

LEADING PROFESSIONALS AND BUSINESS OWNERS

Spirit of Innovation, the first local news and information television show exclusively for Riverside County, and the founder of Digifest Temecula, the city's annual film and media festival. Diane's expertise stems from producing A-list shows like General Hospital, Friends, and Veronica's Closet. She also launched The Disney Channel's Playhouse Disney, worked in the creative division at Universal Studios, and built the High-Def streaming control room at Staples Center for HBO PayPerview and the first national online streaming broadcast for the 2000 Democratic National Convention. Aside from retaining mentionable local clients, including Abbott Vascular, City of Temecula, TEDx, and California State University of San Marcos, Diane is also a community leader serving on the board of multiple organizations such as Riverside County Workforce Development Board and Temecula Valley Chamber of Commerce's Women in Business event. By combining her vast industry experience with her deep involvement in her local community's economic development, she creates opportunities for diverse individuals to gain experience and training for a career in the video production and entertainment industry.

KELLY SCOTT

KELLY SCOTT

CONVERSATION WITH KELLY SCOTT

> Kelly, you are the founder of Kelly Scott Fitness. Tell us about your business and the people that you help.

Kelly Scott: Well, Kelly Scott Fitness has definitely evolved over the past few years. I've been a fitness professional for over 20 years, I started as a group fitness instructor and personal trainer, and I have also owned an outdoor boot camp. I have now shifted my focus to online coaching because it allows me the ability to help more people. I realized my clients needed much more than just a fitness plan; they also needed mindset coaching to help them stay on top of their health and fitness routines. Unfortunately, when life gets hectic, the first thing to go out the window is our self-care. I created my brand to primarily help busy women (though I do have male clients), take back control of their time, energy, and focus, and harness the chaos of life. I still do the online fitness and nutrition pieces. But I've also created a new three-month online coaching course that focuses on time management, self-limiting beliefs, and consistency in schedule so people can stay on top of their self-care routines.

I've brought the important pieces of overall self-care (fitness, nutrition, and mindset) together so that my clients have a few different ways to work with me to help them overcome the struggles they are facing. It's very exciting because my brand has expanded. I'm working on spreading the message that we all have chaos in our lives, but we can't let it take over. We have to be responsible enough to say, "Hey, life is always going to be chaotic. But that is no excuse to neglect my self-care." I teach my clients how to focus on small things they can do throughout the day to create a routine and make life easier.

> **It sounds like you do a lot as a healthy lifestyle coach. In a nutshell, can you explain exactly how people can work with you?**

Kelly Scott: Sure! There are three ways I coach my clients:

1. Nutrition and Fitness
2. Mentoring fitness enthusiasts to start an online business
3. Control Your Chaos Method, my three-month "signature system."

If you are looking for health and fitness coaching, I offer free "healthy formula assessments." On the call, I help you figure out the roadblocks standing in your way of getting the results you seek so that you can live the life you desire. We will work together to get you unstuck and create a sustainable routine to make life easier. You will not only get fit, but you'll also have more energy and stay consistent in your self-care.

If you would like to have more control over your income and have always wanted to learn how to create your own online business, I mentor fitness enthusiasts to get paid to live fit. As healthy lifestyle coaches, we build an online business by reaching our health goals and helping others do the same. I can show you how you can get your fitness paid for, earn a residual online income, and be a part of a community that supports you in life, health, and personal growth. Everything about being a coach on my team can be learned; no experience is necessary. You just need to be coachable, driven, and ready for positive change.

Finally, I have my signature three-month coaching program called "Control Your Chaos." I will teach you how to take control of your time, energy, and focus so you can restore balance and harmony. If you are tired of being pulled in too many directions and feeling overwhelmed with the chaos in life, this is the online program for you! It has it all, including a simple 12-week fitness and nutrition challenge that will help ease you into a self-care routine.

I will include a free gift for the readers to download at the end of this chapter.

I created a special worksheet that will help you keep calm in the chaos. I think you'll love it! I share some of my favorite tips for restoring energy, managing time, and staying focused. Head over to www.kellyscottfitness.com/book to download your free gift. I hope it helps you take some control over the chaos in your life.

> **We're starting to see the light at the end of the tunnel regarding the pandemic. Many people are working out at home with virtual trainers. Have you seen a surge of people wanting online fitness?**

Kelly Scott: I have seen a surge of people wanting to go online. But unfortunately, in my profession, there are always obstacles that I have to help my clients overcome. In most cases, it is the excuse of "not having enough time." With the pandemic, especially in families with children, it's been even more chaotic because they've been thrown into a brand new routine. Most people aren't used to working from home while having their kids distance learning. This has created more obstacles for parents trying to find time for themselves. It is hard to juggle being a parent 24-7 and also managing work, homeschooling, and Zoom calls. Even though there has been a surge in online fitness, I hear more excuses than usual. I help my clients discover the power of a solid, sustainable morning routine where you take care of yourself first and push past those excuses. People that start working with me often think they have to make multiple drastic changes all at once. But that's not the case; I like to take it one step at a time. We pick something to focus on first, whether it be mindset, fitness, or nutrition. When one piece of the puzzle becomes a habit, we can move on to the next part.

> **Do people actively seek you out knowing they need help with mindset?**

Kelly Scott: The importance of improving mindset was a discovery that I made on my own journey of controlling the chaos in my life. I was never one of those people that knew I needed it either. As I've been on my personal development journey, I have incorporated that piece more and more into my coaching.

Let's face it...nobody is perfect. We all have bad days, but we have to learn ways to move forward without letting our setbacks turn into bad weeks, bad months, or even bad years. We have to give ourselves grace and accept that times are different and more challenging. Don't get me wrong, bad days will happen, but what's important is how you learn from those failures/mistakes/setbacks and how quickly you move forward.

> **What are the most common limiting beliefs preventing people from rising to the occasion and getting in shape?**

Kelly Scott: Time is a big limiting belief. People have the misconception that they need to completely rearrange their schedules or dedicate hours to care for themselves. Now that I exercise from home, I literally save hours a week. I head out to my garage gym, choose a workout online, and am done in 30 minutes.

Long gone are the days of needing to spend an hour at the gym to get into shape. Working out from home is a great way to save time, take out the guesswork of what exercises to do, and avoid the typical gym distractions (parking, lines, locker room gossip, etc.). My clients have found that working out at home allows them to enjoy the ability to have some quiet "me time."

Many people also tend to focus on things that haven't worked for them in the past. They think, "Well, if it didn't work for me then, why would I be successful now?" There are many options in the fitness industry to choose from that don't produce lasting results, such as fad diets. I call myself a healthy lifestyle coach because I don't want people to stress about eating right or working out; it should just become part of their natural day. I advise my clients to be open to new things and take one step at a time. I talked with a client the other day who was struggling to fit it all in. I asked her what part would make her feel the best right now, and she chose the nutrition piece. I said, "Awesome, let's do that! In four weeks, we will check back in and add in online workouts." Stressing out by trying to do it all at once isn't necessary and often leads to people giving up. The fact is, if you decide to make a small change in your health, you will automatically feel better, right? It's all about consistency over time. You will start to develop belief in your ability to succeed, lose some weight, eat healthier foods and begin to create healthy habits. It all counts as long as you are moving forward each step of the way.

> **What inspired you to become a fitness coach?**

Kelly Scott: When I was a little kid, my dad would take me to the gym, and I would watch him work out. That was always his lifestyle; he was very active and fit. He inspired me and made me passionate about fitness. I got into competitive cheerleading at a very early age and became a cheer coach at 15 years old. I coached competitive cheer and cheered myself for 18 years. I loved keeping my athletes in shape. During practices, I'd have them do a short workout and give them fitness homework to keep them at the top of their game. So it was a natural progression for me to get into fitness coaching. I just have a passion for helping people succeed and do something they didn't think was possible. Health Coaching was never my full-time profession, just something I did on the side. I did what I was supposed to, graduated from college, and got a full-time job with benefits, but I never felt I was fulfilling my passion and purpose. I would show up to the office and think, "Is this really what I want to do for the next 40 or 50 years of my life?" My passion was fitness, yet I was only coaching a few classes here and there. I really wanted to figure out a way to make health coaching my full-time career. So I just went for it! Even though it was scary as heck, I transitioned from office work to become a full-time fitness professional in my late 20s. But I'm glad I took that leap. I have impacted so many lives over the years! It's never too late to change directions and do something you are genuinely passionate about. Life is too short to be stuck at a 9-5 job that you dread going to and only get excited for the weekends.

> **What would you say to people on the fence about making positive changes towards their fitness, nutrition, and overall health?**

Kelly Scott: If you want to experience change, you have to alter something in your daily routine. Change is always scary, and it can be hard. But when you step into the "hard" and embrace the "hard," that is when your life can really start changing. You can't be afraid to step out of your comfort zone. If you are feeling comfortable where you're at, you are probably not pushing yourself hard enough. No matter where you're at in life, whether you are working with me or someone else, know that being pushed and being uncomfortable are things you should always be striving for. I was in my comfort zone for a long time, and I was really unhappy until I realized that challenge and change are good things. Nothing is impossible when it comes to your health, fitness, and career goals. You just have to take that first step and decide that now is the time and don't look back.

KELLY SCOTT

Healthy Lifestyle Coach, Founder of Kelly Scott Fitness

Kelly is a successful entrepreneur and has been in the fitness industry since 1998. She started her coaching career at the young age of 15 as a competitive cheerleading coach.

In 2009 Kelly retired from cheerleading to focus on her fitness career. About a year later, she transitioned from working in the fitness industry part-time to full-time, a long-term goal that she finally achieved.

Now she offers online health coaching, fitness accountability groups, and a three-month signature program called "Control Your Chaos." Kelly helps hundreds of people a year reach their health goals through time-saving fitness programs, easy-to-follow nutrition plans, and ongoing accountability.

Kelly is the CEO and Founder of Kelly Scott Fitness and EmpowerFIT, the Founder of The Empowered Nation Coaching Team, a Certified Personal Trainer, a Master Nutrition Coach, Healthy Lifestyle Coach, and Business Mentor.

Kelly is passionate about helping others take control of their health by creating simple, sustainable daily routines that will help make life easier.

Be sure to sign up for your free gift! Kelly put together a worksheet with her top tips for restoring energy, managing time, and staying focused. Use the link below to grab it now!

FREE GIFT:
https://www.kellyscottfitness.com/book

WEBSITE:
https://www.kellyscottfitness.com/

EMAIL:
kelly@kellyscottfitness.com

FACEBOOK:
https://www.facebook.com/coachkellyscott

INSTAGRAM HANDLE:
@coachkellyscott

LINKEDIN:
https://www.linkedin.com/in/coachkellyscott/

JENNY AMBROSE

JENNY AMBROSE

CONVERSATION WITH JENNY AMBROSE

> Jenny, you are the founder of Purée Fantastico and an award-winning artist and designer for business. Tell us about your company and the people you serve.

Jenny Ambrose: Purée Fantastico is a blend of design, anthropology, emotional intelligence, and critical thinking. I realized that design needs grounding, intention, and direction for it to be trackable and efficient. I serve fortune five hundred companies, art universities, and thousands of independent businesses across the globe. I've even worked with the German government. Whether it be burlesque dancers, financial planners, educational pursuits, or makeup artists, it doesn't matter to me. What matters is… "What are we doing? What are we saying? How do we want our customers to feel?"

> **What is the number one challenge your clients face?**

Jenny Ambrose: Self-acceptance. I work with people who haven't seen what they want to bring into the world. They might be frustrated because nobody else gets them. That is why I started Purée Fantastico. My clients immediately feel at ease when I say, "Whatever you want to make happen, it's possible. It's possible."

> **What are some common myths and misconceptions your clients have about marketing their business?**

Jenny Ambrose: A common misconception is that you need a billion-dollar logo or brand right out of the gate, or even in six months. It is not possible because you don't have the backend information and knowledge to do it with comfort and confidence. Not only that, these things won't help you to grow and figure it out. As entrepreneurs, we put so much unnecessary pressure on ourselves, and I tell my clients that right away.

> **What does the process look like when a client decides to work with you?**

Jenny Ambrose: My process is the same whether I am making a business name, demographic market strategy, visual brand, or package design. I send the client a questionnaire that ranges from the practical to the abstract because I want to see who I'm working with, how they view their problems, and what they want to bring into the world. I study this information and guide them through verbal and visual inspiration. For example, someone could show me a Wendy's ad because they like how something was phrased or find the color palette appealing. It all depends on what the client sees and what speaks to them. We take so much for granted regarding what we experience, what that means to us, and how we want to use it. After this in-depth conversation, I offer my creative solutions.

> **What are some mistakes that people make with their messaging or branding that you can help them avoid?**

Jenny Ambrose: I see many logos that are very specialized and detailed and contain a lot of elements that don't need to be there. Instead, you should be focusing on the whole brand. When you have a logo that is more like an art piece, it ties you into something you can't grow with. For example, my logo is very clean and structured. The rest of it is fun and colorful, but the letters are boring. And because those letters are boring, I can grow and add and build on those to create a fun brand.

The other mistake is doing things because "you think you should." That is the number one marketing killer. The magic sauce is YOU! It doesn't matter what other coaches or financial planners are doing. What do YOU want to do? Because if there were someone already doing it that way, you wouldn't exist in that space. So make *that* the space you exist in, the space you already inhabit.

> Tell us about "Purée Fantastico." How did you come up with the name?

Jenny Ambrose: One of the very first projects I ever had the opportunity to work on ended up being published in a design manual. I took it from a simple design project to a design strategy marketing experience that changed the game for the Art Institute I was going to. I was so excited, and it was a big deal to me. And I'm looking through print magazines thinking to myself, "How can I ever tell people about all the things I can do?" Out of nowhere, "Purée Fantastico" comes into my brain. And I thought maybe I heard it in a song somewhere. But no...it was my own creation! So I bought the domain name and set up my Etsy shop back in 2008. Design is my passion. Anthropology is my life's blood. I really love these things. And when I would try to get a full-time job, it was very difficult. People would look at my portfolio and say, "You're so talented, and we just love you. But you won't be happy here." Nobody teaches you how to counter that. So when the economy crashed in 2008, I decided to do things a different way. I love what I do, and I never gave up on it. That's why I've had the opportunity to serve so many different people.

> **How does anthropology connect to marketing and advertising?**

Jenny Ambrose: It's two sides of the same coin for me. How do the roots connect to the flower? Anthropology is an all-consuming passion of mine. I watch commercials to figure out what archetype they're using to sell to me, and I just love it. In art school, I realized, "Oh, anthropology IS this." It is the visuals we see and the invisible thing that we are all speaking to, pulling from, and blending together. Design is about connection and communication. Anthropology is what is being communicated and connected. In my experience, that is not viewed as the same. Instead of being angry, I'm like, "Oh, I'll just show you. I know how this works. I'll just show you." For me, it is about changing the culture of design by bringing in anthropology, algebra, and geometry (some of my favorite things). But I'm also changing the culture by helping people speak to the clients they want to talk to in a way that connects to them. It's not the re-embodiment of the 1980s corporate mindset. It's reworking that and saying that's not going to work for everyone. Here's how you can still be professional. Here's how you can still make sense. Here's how you can track that and make that effort work.

> **What inspired you to get started in design?**

Jenny Ambrose: Honestly, I feel like I'm creativity and emotion with skin put on top. At 18 months, I was wriggling out of my crib, going downstairs, turning on *Sesame Street*, and drawing at the table for HOURS. That evolved into making my own dolls and writing my own stories. At eight years old, I turned my entire basement into an art studio. It's just who I am. And I did not realize people had careers in design. I was forever obsessed with letters; I broke every dot-matrix printer we had growing up, writing letters to my friends and making every word a different font. I was obsessed with language and culture. My parents were in theater. And my mother would bring home foreign films all of the time. I remember sitting behind the couch past bedtime, listening to them speak Mandarin or Portuguese and just being fascinated with the sounds.

I've always been a curious, learning-obsessed, creative individual. Of course, design is going to make sense for me. Design takes all of the things and all of the curiosity and says, "Here you go. Now you make sense of other things." Growing up, I made my own T-shirts for *Nirvana*. People would come up to me and say, "I love your shirt. Where can I buy it?" I made my own stickers for bands that didn't make stickers. And I was getting notes on my car that read, "I love this sticker. Where can I buy it?" So at 18 or 19 years old, I said to myself, "I guess I'm going to do this." At the time, I was going to school for anthropology, and I was asked to be on an archeological dig in Chichen Itza. I got accepted into design school the same week. So I chose design school. And the rest is history. I was like, "Oh, you mean I can make posters using algebra to explain the film *Magnolia*? GREAT! You mean I can make a calendar using all the different philosophies between the Greek and Roman times? AMAZING!" Design was a way for me to explain how I understood the world in a visual, strategic way.

> How can people who resonate with your message find you and connect with you?

Jenny Ambrose: My website is puréefantastico.com. You can also find me on Facebook or Instagram at Purée Fantastico.

JENNY AMBROSE

Founder of Purée Fantastico

Jenny Ambrose is an award-winning designer, creative, and innovative thinker running an award-winning design science & strategy studio, Purée Fantastico. She's worked with large Fortune 500's such as Old Navy, HSN, POPSUGAR, ELLE, American Greetings, Alaskan Airlines, 3M, Charles Schwab, Walgreens, Reuters, and thousands more across the last 15 years,

LEADING PROFESSIONALS AND BUSINESS OWNERS

She's taken large Fortune 500 businesses from 5M to 500M in revenue, boosted an art school's attendance from 33%-77%, and increased her small business client's inquiries from 2x-14x.

Part scientist, part artist, all powerhouse, Jenny knows how to sync with her client's deepest voice and concerns and communicate the solutions as if they'd always been present (because they are!).

Whether it's creative direction, design, illustration, copywriting, strategic problem solving, or thorough research and analysis, it can be trusted that Jenny can handle it with grace, tireless expertise, and unstoppable enthusiasm.

-"Holy cow, how many amazing things can I say about Jenny? How much space do I have here? Definitely not enough."

-"Open, giving, fanatical perfectionist, excellent communicator, talented, and an uncanny ability to perfectly tune her skills to whatever project you throw at her."

-"I am not an easy person to work with, and she never skipped a beat."

-"She knows how to listen, give feedback, and act precisely, moving a project forward on budget and on time. She's amazing and worth every penny she quotes you. And probably then some."

-David Zeitz

-"Jenny is a design goddess. From the moment we started working on an intellectually stringent job that required not just beautiful work but smart, keen – at times, mathematical – prowess, she delivered. She provided option after option. She did so with enthusiasm. She was game. A goddess, I tell you. A rare find."

-Dawn DeKeyser

WEBSITE:
www.pureefantastico.com

EMAIL:
info@pureefantastico.com

FACEBOOK:
www.facebook.com/pureefantastico

INSTAGRAM:
www.instagram.com/pureefantastico

LINKEDIN:
www.linkedin.com/company/pureefantastico

SHOWLEH TOLBERT

SHOWLEH TOLBERT

CONVERSATION WITH SHOWLEH TOLBERT

> **Showleh, you are the founder of NLP Success Coaches. Tell us about your business and the people that you help.**

Showleh Tolbert: Have you ever wanted to get better? We're the company that shows people how to get better faster by creating permanent positive changes in their lives. We teach people how to get the results they want and model excellence in their professional or personal lives. We do that through neuro-linguistic programming. Time Line Therapy® is utilized to get rid of past negative emotions and limiting beliefs that we have. We also implement hypnosis to install positive changes within ourselves. NLP coaching involves learning about how to coach yourself and others to get desired results.

> **Can you define NLP?**

Showleh Tolbert: NLP is not something new or invented. Various techniques are based on studying excellent behaviors, excellent ways of thinking, and excellent strategies. The goal is to model excellence and install it within yourself and others. NLP is a process rather than content. How do I do what I do? How do I change? What needs to be changed? How do I recognize there is something that needs to be changed? It is like rewiring your brain's neurology to produce the results you want in the shortest amount of time. In other words, NLP is how to use the language of the mind to achieve our specific and desired outcomes consistently.

> **Can you give us an example of something people inadvertently do and what can be done to rewire it?**

Showleh Tolbert: Procrastination. People sit on something for months and months, lacking the motivation to do what needs to be done. There is a technique in NLP that teaches you how to stop procrastinating forever. Any time you want to accomplish something, you will become motivated to start it or finish it, resulting in a feeling of accomplishment. People tend to have 1,000 reasons why they shouldn't do something. This technique helps to get rid of the reasons why you shouldn't do something and focuses on results and why you should.

> **How do you implement NLP? What is the process?**

Showleh Tolbert: First of all, we get you to understand yourself. For example, when someone says something to you, what is it that you do in your mind that produces the behavior, reaction, or results you have? This is more than our self-talk. What pictures are you creating in your mind? What are you focusing on? What are you feeling? How are you translating information that comes through unconscious filters? We teach techniques to bring these things from an unconscious to a conscious level to make changes. Once you make the changes, it becomes unconscious once again. Whenever people think about wanting to change a bad habit, they try to do it consciously. Perhaps you want to stop twirling your hair. Deliberately, you would say to yourself, "Stop twirling the hair. I should stop this right now." NLP takes away that consciousness and gives you other behaviors to replace it with. When changes are made at the unconscious level, they occur very quickly. NLP aims to discover the root cause of our behaviors. If you drive down the road and typically prefer right turns, NLP helps you develop the neurology to go to the left.

> **How quickly do your clients see results?**

Showleh Tolbert: For something like procrastination, the technique takes only 5 to 10 minutes. Suppose we are talking about negative emotions that stem from childhood experiences. In that case, the Time Line Therapy® technique takes 5 to 7 minutes for each negative emotion, and you are immediately relieved of all the negative emotions such as anger, sadness, fear, hurt, and guilt. The more you let go, the faster your unconscious mind can let go. We also see clients who have limiting beliefs holding them back. "I want to make more money. I want to be happy. I want more confidence. I'm not enough." These are all examples of limiting beliefs. NLP and Time Line Therapy® can rectify these in 5 to 10 minutes.

> **What types of people benefit from learning NLP?**

Showleh Tolbert: NLP is not just about doing it for yourself, but about helping others. Coaches, lawyers, doctors, real estate agents, CEOs, and other people working in teams need to know how to motivate their team. How do they get the best results from their team? How do they make everyone productive? How do they increase communication? Once you learn NLP, you can comprehend how a particular person talks to themselves. You can then match your communication to their style of communication and increase their level of understanding. Parents who want to teach their children "how to think" and not "what to think" also benefit from NLP. It is especially important in this day and age when everything is changing so rapidly. How do you navigate through life? What information do you allow to enter your mind? How do you have to think to get results?

NLP has also been used in business and marketing significantly. Politicians and presidents are trained in NLP, how to communicate to a group of people, have people join their quest (whatever that quest may be), and how to change people's mindsets. NLP has been around since the 70s, but not many people knew about it. However, in today's information age, the term "NLP" is becoming widely known, and people can identify those that have been trained in NLP by their ability to create positive solutions.

What is Time Line Therapy®?

Showleh Tolbert: Dr. Tad James created Time Line Therapy®, and it is practiced all over the world. It is a combination of NLP and hypnosis. It allows you to let go of what is holding you back in your life, find the root cause of your negative emotions, limiting beliefs, or internal conflicts, get positive learnings, and then let go of the negative emotion. Everyone has a timeline.

It is a collection of memories that can impact where we are today. Time Line Therapy® is a content-free process meaning we don't allow the client to relive the bad memories. Time Line Therapy® is not talk therapy, and when I work with the client, the only thing I know is the negative emotion that I am working on releasing for them.

> **How long does it take for someone to become a certified coach?**

Showleh Tolbert: At the practitioner level, it's seven days of training, and the students get four certifications including, NLP Practitioner, Time Line Therapy® Practitioner, Hypnosis, and NLP Life Coach.

> **When you coach using these techniques, how long does it take to eliminate a particular problem?**

Showleh Tolbert: Well, it depends. A breakthrough takes anywhere from 6 to 10 hours. Addiction is about 12 hours, and PTSD is about 4 to 5 hours. I would say the average is 4 to 10 hours depending on the complexity of the issue.

> **What inspired you to get into NLP?**

Showleh Tolbert: I've always been on a mission to make myself better, especially being a mother. I would look around at others who had such poise and confidence and wanted to know how they made it look so effortless. One of those people mentioned NLP to me. The researcher in me went to work, and I decided I wanted to learn it for myself. I have a very scientific mind, and I liked that these were science-based techniques; tried, effective, and producing results. I wasn't planning on becoming a coach. I simply wanted to do it for personal development. But as I learned more and more, I became passionate about getting this knowledge out to as many people as possible. So I became a trainer in NLP, Time Line Therapy®, a Hypnotherapist, and instructor of Hypnotherapy and made a career out of it. Besides teaching NLP, I am a master coach and work with clients to let go of what is holding them back from achieving results.

> **For anyone who resonates with your message and wants to learn more, how can they find you and connect with you?**

Showleh Tolbert: My website is NLPsuccesscoaches.com. You can also connect with me via phone at 949-522-1615. I am on Facebook at Coach Showleh and Instagram at NLP Success

Coaches. I provide a free, half-hour consultation to see if NLP is a good fit for you. We will spend the time talking, whether you want to learn NLP or get rid of issues such as depression or PTSD. Perhaps you just want a better life and to free yourself of limitations. People have to believe and want to change to experience it. I cannot force anyone to change. I hope that you will reach out and embrace getting rid of whatever is holding you back.

SHOWLEH TOLBERT

Master Coach, Founder of NLP Success Coaches

Showleh Tolbert is a board-certified Hypnotherapist, Master Coach, and trainer of Neuro-Linguistic Programming (NLP), Time Line Therapy®, instructor of Hypnotherapy and NLP Life Coaching. She is the founder of nlpsuccesscoaches.com, an accredited international Coaching and Training Academy providing certification programs through ABNLP, TLT®, ABH, Coaching Division of ABNLP boards.

LEADING PROFESSIONALS AND BUSINESS OWNERS

Showleh is passionate about getting positive results. She coaches her clients in a way that utilizes both their heads and their hearts creating solutions to achieve their personal and professional goals. The techniques she has mastered are the latest scientific technologies in the field of coaching and accelerated human development. Showleh is highly trained in modalities, taking her clients from where they are at to where they want to be in the shortest amount of time, creating permanent positive changes in their lives. She takes great pride and joy in the progress and success of her clients and students.

Showleh has over 30 years of experience at executive levels both in the corporate and public sectors. She has a BA in Finance, Masters in Business, and is currently pursuing her PhD. Before starting her training and coaching business, she was the executive director of an international charity organization for children with cancer. Showleh is a survivor of a domestic violence relationship, thus her passion for helping others. Her mission is to transform the planet one person at a time. The legacy Showleh would like to leave behind is making a positive difference in the lives of others.

Showleh's hobbies are playing chess, reading, traveling, and exploring different cultures. She loves taking long walks and meditating. Showleh is now married, has a daughter, and lives with her husband and their rescued Costa Rican dog in Irvine, CA.

WEBSITE:
http://www.nlpsuccesscoaches.com

PHONE:
949-522-1615

EMAIL:
showleh@nlpsuccesscoaches.com

FACEBOOK:
https://www.facebook.com/coachshowleh

INSTAGRAM:
https://www.instagram.com/nlpsuccesscoaches/

LINKEDIN:
https://www.linkedin.com/in/showleh/

ABOUT THE PUBLISHER

Mark Imperial is a Best-Selling Author, Syndicated Business Columnist, Syndicated Radio Host, and internationally recognized Stage, Screen, and Radio Host of numerous business shows spotlighting leading experts, entrepreneurs, and business celebrities.

His passion is to discover noteworthy business owners, professionals, experts, and leaders who do great work and share their stories and secrets to their success with the world on his syndicated radio program titled "Remarkable Radio."

Mark is also the media marketing strategist and voice for some of the world's most famous brands. You can hear his voice over the airwaves weekly on Chicago radio and worldwide on iHeart Radio.

Mark is a Karate black belt, teaches kickboxing, loves Thai food, House Music, and his favorite TV shows are infomercials.

Learn more:

www.MarkImperial.com
www.ImperialAction.com
www.RemarkableRadioShow.com